BOA
EDITIONS
LIMITED

*Desire Lines*

# Desire Lines:
# New and Selected Poems

## LOLA HASKINS

AMERICAN POETS CONTINUUM SERIES, NO. 84

BOA Editions, Ltd.   •   Rochester, NY   •   2004

First Edition
04 05 06 07   7 6 5 4 3 2 1

Publications by BOA Editions, Ltd.—
a not-for-profit corporation under section 501 (c) (3)
of the United States Internal Revenue Code—
are made possible with the assistance of grants from
the Literature Program of the New York State Council on the Arts,
the Literature Program of the National Endowment for the Arts,
the Sonia Raiziss Giop Charitable Foundation,
the Lannan Foundation,
as well as from the Mary S. Mulligan Charitable Trust,
the County of Monroe, NY,
the Rochester Area Community Foundation,
Ames-Amzalak Memorial Trust,
and The CIRE Foundation.

See Colophon on page 160 for special individual acknowledgments.

Cover Design:  Lisa Mauro/Mauro Design
Cover Art: "Japonesque" by Norman Jensen
Interior Design and Composition: Richard Foerster
Manufacturing: McNaughton & Gunn
BOA Logo: Mirko

Library of Congress Cataloging-in-Publication Data

Haskins, Lola.
  Desire lines : new and selected poems / Lola Haskins.— 1st ed.
     p. cm. — (American poets continuum series ; v. 84)
  Includes bibliographical references.
  ISBN 1–929918–49–6 (pbk.)
  I. Title. II. Series.

PS3558.A7238D47 2004
811'.54—dc22

                                                        2004004422

NATIONAL
ENDOWMENT
FOR THE ARTS

NYSCA

BOA Editions, Ltd.
Thom Ward, Editor
H. Allen Spencer, Chair
A. Poulin, Jr., President & Founder (1938–1996)
260 East Avenue, Rochester, NY 14604
www.boaeditions.org

# Contents

*from* PLANTING THE CHILDREN
(1983)

# Nursery Rhyme: Numbers

Seven old ladies
   crochet
      for the boys.

Six old ladies
   hear thunder.

Five old ladies
   afraid
      of the noise.

Four old ladies
   go under.

One old lady
   to pick up
      the lace.

One old lady
   is crying.

How cruel
   to be born
      with only

one face
   and to see

in the mirror
   its
      dying.

# Grandmother Speaks of the Old Country

That year there were many deaths in the village.
Germs flew like angels from one house to the next
and every family gave up its own. Mothers
died at their mending. Children fell at school.
Of three hundred twenty, there were eleven left.
Then, quietly, the sun set on a day when no one
died. And the angels whispered among themselves.
And that evening, as he sat on the stone steps,
your grandfather felt a small wind on his neck
when all the trees were still. And he would tell us
always, how he had felt that night, on the skin
of his own neck, the angels, passing.

# Aquarium

Here behind glass they are stacked
in schools. Far from the leaping cold
of Iceland, cod wait without their hearts.
Here, headless shrimp crowd together.
Here are salmon, carved in flat lyres,
that we may know them by their color only.
And look, children, here are the smelts.
They have left them whole.
Do you think, if we take them home
and thaw them out, they will show us
what it was like to swim, thick as shoppers,
down the dark aisles of the sea?

## Children, Stop Us

Children, stop us.
We are running
away with you.
Soon you will
forget the shore,
and how birds
used to sound
at morning.
Stop us.
We're unfurling
our sails
like flags and
will whisk you
on the breeze
away from yourselves.
Hold your breaths.
Do not let it happen.
When we send you
flowers, refuse.
When we mention
how fresh the wind
feels on a high sea,
do not listen.
When we go down
to our long boats,
say goodbye.

*from* CASTINGS
(1984)

# In each of my fingers

In each of my fingers is another woman.
The hairs on my head
belonged to someone else.
Their ends are split with their long history.
Sometimes my feet carry me
where Jane wanted to go, where Ann
dreamed in her tower.
I am Ellen out of her century.
The way girls bare their legs
shames my thee-saying heart.
When I speak, I hear harmonies
I do not understand.
But other ladies flow in me like blood.
Their other lives swell
the veins on the backs of my hands.
Their stories scatter like black bees
from my mouth, and return
to lie with me through the dangerous night.

# If you stroke my back

If you stroke my back, it is Ann you touch,
who never felt the fingers of her king so gently,
but opens now her body against greasy bones
and lying voices at chapel.
She has come far, who used to put on
her morning petticoats atremble, in hopes
no call would come to his canopied bed
where, like a eunuch, she performed for him
acts she sang against in the dark.
And if we love each other well,
it will be her heart's red beating you feel
against your chest, her heart
from her body which was taken away
but now returns. But if I tell you no
you must understand
that the damp and the rats and the licey hay
on which I sleep are more than I can bear.
I will not be long. Wait for me.

# Speaking with Lucy (d. 1736): Her Answers

When I was eight.
The fever.
Leeches. Ugh! Flat gray mouths against my stomach.
The doctor held me down.
I screamed for you.
Because you had not been born.
Because I would not grow up to say what mattered.
Because you can.

# A Study in Time

There is a door. There is a woman.
The woman sits in a blue chair and will not
go through the door.
She does not imagine, on the other side,
her child's body
in a plain box on her only table.

The woman is watching a woodpecker
whose quick beak snatches beetles from the dead
oak in the yard.
She is thinking of the pounding in her head
under the smooth braids. She is thinking
of the rot in the heart of the tree.

The woman starts towards the door.
Her child bursts in, an acorn in his fat fist.
*Mama Mama, look what I found!*
The tree falls on the house.

The woman opens the door.
On the table she sets one plate.
White, shining.

# from *Julia Stranahan (1880–1970)*

## *Thoughts While Teaching Grammar*

Coming to school this morning along the hoed path,
holding my skirts above the green-slicked water,
something unusual, an omen. A fat-ruffed turkey
gobbled in my way, not crossing but standing,
shaking his fanned tail for a mate. When I tried
to pass, he hurried ahead, displaying again,
insisting. His urgent feathers rattled, leading
all other sound. I stepped forward then and
answered him, fanning my skirt fast, wrists
vibrating like wing-stubs. His claw feet stepped
back. He spread and shook. I ran at him, waving
wild skirts. He broke away into palmettos.
The children are staring. I am repeating a lesson
they had word-perfect long ago. They do not understand.

## Imagined Family Photograph: Double Exposure

He will stand by me, his hand resting like a bird
on my shoulder. I will be wearing my best poplin,
which the camera will alter from blue to black.
The children will be there too, the girls
in their white frocks sitting, the boys standing.
It will be difficult to say how many children,
because at the moment the picture happens
they will move, dissolved at some joke
which Frank and I either have not heard
or must ignore. This is years from now.
Or: Frank sits, I stand.
There is only one child, a thin-faced girl.
The ghosts of her brothers and sisters
are looking over her shoulder. She
does not see them, but I do. *Stop, ghosts,*
I am telling them. But they titter and
push to get into the picture. Frank is wax.
His image and the child's are sharp.
Mine is blurred. Behind me white curtains blow,
though afterwards we said we could not remember
a day so still. Tornado weather, we said,
but no tornado came.

# The Phonograph Arrives, 1904

Frank's Pride we called it when it came,
lashed beside the driver on the early stage.
We lifted it from its splintered seat
and placed it in the best corner of the post.
Then, we unpacked the wax cylinders, set in
tissue paper, like eggs, by careful fingers
in New York, and we read their legends:
*The Stars and Stripes Forever, Dora, My Wild
Irish Rose.*

      (Later we named it Devon, for the boy
we didn't have, imagining its songs his voice,
calling to the parakeets in the thicket, and
the parakeets answering. But before we could
finish, Billy Tommy came to trade, brought otter,
egret feathers, and eleven fine alligator hides,
at ten cents the inch. He asked for calico and salt,
and grits, and a shiny new pot for the food
his woman tended. While he chose, she wandered,
fingering cheesecloth, pouring beads from hand to hand,
two children clinging to her ribboned skirt
puckered on each side by their dark fingers.
*Oh Frank*, I said, *play one now. Billy won't mind.*
So Frank looked up from his red and yellow bolt,
his yardstick in his hand, and then he played
our first song, the first recording in Fort Lauderdale,
and it was *The Stars and Stripes Forever.*

There were hides everywhere. Feathers floated like sneezes
as Billy's children ran for the door. As he herded
the last child out, Billy stopped. *Canned man*, he said.
*Me no like canned man.* And the grand march played on,
and we never laughed at Billy, not even when
his dugout was long gone around the farthest bend.
We had our particular music in those days, and we
wore it as I wore my long skirts, even in the heat,
and my high-necked blouses buttoned to my throat.

# The white curtains blow

The white curtains blow like ghosts.
For a moment the wind holds its breath and then
hard rain nails pelt the tin.
By the dimpling river, Frank is tying
his raft to a tree. Twice he wraps the rope
(he has lost rafts before).
And again. Then one slow knot
and then he turns.
I see him starting up the slope.
I hold the door open.
But the leaves rise up and throw themselves
at him. His knife drives down
like a scream. I run. *Get the hoe, woman!*
He is rubbing his leg with both thick hands.
By his foot a snub head writhes against
the knife. Frank chops at it. It severs. Released,
the body twists once, like an impossible arm.
Frank's shirt sleeves stream. He leans on me.
Like a courting couple we walk together
towards the house. The screen door bangs,
again and again, like someone who cannot stop talking
because there is nothing he can say.

## Nightly he pumps at my dry well

Nightly he pumps at my dry well like a desperate
man who knows the water witch lied
but drills and drills because he paid.
Since his leg healed and he knew
he would not die, he has blamed me.
Each sullen forkful thrust in his mouth
says, *Where is the child?*
And every month my blood betrays me again
with its red slap. At the post I take
their money, the money of women
with babies on their hips.
They do not even count their change.

# Teaching the Miccosukkee: Later

The Medicine Man at Big Cypress hates me.
He has sliced Annie's ears.
Others come now, but the children of Big Cypress
look down when they see me at the post.
With his potion of nettle and bitter oak
the Medicine Man has shriveled
the child I would have grown.
In dreams he tells me what he has done.

The Medicine Man at Big Cypress buys nothing here.
Others come, with their pigs and their dogs
and their chickens with muddy feathers.
The Medicine Man stays in his chickee,
built with none of our nails,
sharpening his knives for little ears.
They cannot keep the knowledge from him.
Let an ibis cross the swamp
five miles away, ten miles,
and he knows.

## On Their Opposition to Education

> *When an Indian learns to read and write, he learns to lie.*
> —Water Turkey

I have told you about the children, how I tried
to shape their mouths, how I carried to them,
in my two hands, my God. But He spilled
through my fingers and one day they said,
*Lady, you bring us nothing.* And it was true.
Two learned to write their names and one
to read the paper he'd filled with the one word.
But the names they wrote
were not the ones they owned.
And the saints I taught them
those men turned pale at the root
from too much washing, these too failed.
It is as if I am crouched outside the circle
of the fire at their camp up the slough,
insect wings brushing my bitten face.
The children I saw today
have different names tonight.
And the babies lie in their mothers' laps
with tiny flames in their eyes
while their brothers and sisters speak,
on and on in the language I never learned.
Then the frogs and cicadas grow suddenly loud
like a speeding heart.
And they all turn towards me.

# from *Jane Marshall (1835–1910)*

## Dedication: Lola to Jane

For months we have lived together, you a blond
light under my dark skin. And when you tell me
stories, they are dreams I had before I was born,
and I am saying, *Yes. This is how it was.*
The trees cast such complicated shadows
on our dirt floor. On my lap is the orange jar
Winston brought you from Richmond, the one
you kept filled with hickory nuts. But now
your voice trails off, like a dusk bird
vanishing into deeper woods. You are leaving me.
Your gold warmth is fading in my arms
and, Jane, I want you to stay. But the sun's
too low, and we live in different times.
No matter what we do, the cold comes in.

## *I may not yet write*

I may not yet write, for you are too lately
lost, have no place now where an envelope
might find a home. Yet there is much to do.
I must wake my pen from its long dry sleep,
must walk the round words, like babies,
across the page, must nurse them for
the hard tasks which will be their lot
too soon, for they must learn, before
they are grown, how to keep a man alive.
And there are things I would have them
tell you: how our new child grows, happy
and swelling in his sisters' house.
And there are things I would have them
never say: how your bayonet sliced
my eyes today as it shone, bright
as a woman in the morning river sun.

## *Surely there must be others*


Surely there must be others, other wives
whose men wear gray and have been long
from home, others who wake flushed as I.
Surely somewhere a Margaret rubs, as if
by chance, against the spindle at which
she works her skirts pouring blue
to the floor. And somewhere, surely,
a Mary lies alone, her thighs pressed
tighter to the sheets than if she slept.
I have kept silence with my heart before,
folded it like a bird into a locket
snapped shut. But this silence is
some other. It flies through gold.
In the cold night the clock strikes four.
Even the roof moans in the dawn wind.

## My fingers are mending

My fingers are mending. Yellow mouths
close in Becky's hem as the thin lady
flies, weaving her hair into
the cloth.
        My lap is the place,
the valley for hurt dresses, a home
for socks that cannot go on.
Here come garments like petitioners,
and are made whole with the only thread
there is. We all go about these days
bearing white puckered scars, and yet
still we say Good Morning and,
at length, Good Night. In my head
I am writing this down. In my
head, I am taking my new nightdress
out of the box, and my dear,
it was quite the perfect present.
It takes the light whitely
and shines like needles.

## Becky's in the sweet corn running

Becky's in the sweet corn running.
Here and there I glimpse her yellow
dress between the rows, parted neatly
as a negro's head. Now she calls out:
*Hide and Seek!*
We can hear the guns.
Ours or theirs, we cannot tell,
nor who may come marching
over the planted hill.

(Dream)

## Robbie coughs blood roses

Robbie coughs blood roses in his crib.
I grease his shaking chest with salve,
but fear I can only ease his going
for hourly he slides away. The day
shines blue in the window. A little
breeze does the best it can. I mind
the child. In his wrinkled face
his death blooms slowly.

## Winston, you were wrong

Winston, you were wrong to dance in such a place.
Since the news came to my ears,
I have pictured you countless times,
a cavorting great bear, with her rouged
hand in yours, and she flinging up
her skirts. And that Belle standing by
the while, her fat arms folded. And then,
slurring, you turn your pockets inside out
and hand your pay to Belle's red smile
This is a reproof I do not deserve.
You may say I was not there.
You may claim that it was otherwise.
But I will tell you this:
I will withhold my bed from you,
and should you approach me there,
I will wake the children that they may see
what kind of creature they call
Father. I am sending this by Alan.
He says you go to battle soon.

## *I have grown plump and settled these months*

I have grown plump and settled these months,
domestic as the white chickens that peck
outside, whose smooth eggs our children
gather in baskets. Yet I must tell you
what I have learned. Inside each egg
is a yellow scream. At night sometimes,
when all the chickens are asleep under
the moon, the eggs shriek in their shells,
wanting something. When I come
from my bed and pick them up,
they quiet, as I rock them in my skirt.

## My dear, today we sold the last pig

My dear, today we sold the last pig, and who
knows when we shall get another. But collards
crowd the garden, hurry into bloom faster than
we can pick, and onions, round as babies' heads
swell daily. So much abundance have we here
that every seed we plant springs eager from
the ground while I sit, for a moment alone,
writing brown lines to a dead man. When I
tell you, *The children have not forgotten
your name*, my fingers scratch against
the page like live things, and the mockingbird
that has been all day singing in the trees,
stops. His wings rustle in the leaves. Then
there is a dark settling and a quiet under
the branches, where the light never comes.

# from *Patsy, Property of George Sherman (1816–1856)*

## *Mama said it was thundering*

Mama said it was thundering when I was born
and can I see it, the rain beating its wings
against the door, the cold bird laughing
up in the clouds, all the blood,
brightest color in the room
when I came out. And she said
there was a caul over my face,
so she couldn't tell at first if I was black,
or white like him. The caul's why
only Chloe plays with me, the others
call me white girl or little princess veil,
but Chloe stays close.
Together we two build our graves,
dreaming great mounds of sand to bury us,
and every night we die,
and every morning rise to life again

## Patsy Sees a Ghost

I'm crossing the river where it narrows,
carefully, it being Sunday
and I'm past the root end of the log
when I look up,
and there's a haunt sitting
on the blossom end.
I can see trumpet vine and blackberries
through her white dress.
Gnats hang in the air.
The river runs, red-brown and deep.
The haunt sings
and it's my music, the blood song
of my Sunday skin, the rattle-tune
of my heart and bones
and my skull dancing in the road.
And Chloe, she knows my name.
She says, *Oh Patsy, take care,*
*or you will surely fall*
*and the thick river*
*will pull you too to shroudy weeds*
*and you'll be gone,*
*gone as the moment you looked up*
*and saw the trumpet vine and*
*berries, hot and ready*
*through my white dress,*
*gone as all the years since I died,*
*and waited here for you.*

## Patsy Speaks of the Master

The sun rises to the driver's horn
as surely as a woman sets her mending down
to follow the man she hates
to his urgent cot across the room.
What starts goes on. Noon sun
blinds those who look, turns pupils
white as mistress' sheets
stretched across the fine high bed
where she lies.
It's my skin her husband tongues,
my black legs he spreads
though I tell him no.
My children will murder hers.
The helpless sun rises, and burns.

## Patsy Jumps over the Broom

### i

Esau says
his master will ask mine for me,
but I don't want him.
When he came after me that day
with his old man's tongue flapping
in his mouth, closer, 'til his turnip breath
was hot against my cheek,
I spat my answer on the stove.

### ii

Master has put me in his pocket.
Sold, my heart rattles in my throat
like desperate coins.

### iii

Chloe's hands flurry through my hair,
quick brown birds through leaves,
flying out oiled
with my scent and the wedding smell
she adds from a milk-white jar.
Her chatter is as far away
as birds in dreams
like little ticking clocks
whose time
is happening to someone else.
I buy my master for fifty dollars.
He is begging me,
take my wife too, my son,

my daughter's young and strong.
I pay him no attention.


## iv


Esau and I stand together facing the broom.
It is all I see
though the room's bright with women's dresses.
Its straws that once had roots
are choked by dust and broken insects,
teased from corners.
Its handle, cut from some tree's heart,
is mute and dirty.
I can change nothing,
must cross this border.
And on the other side,
Esau will have won
what I wanted not to give.
Already I hear
his branched whip's crack,
opening channels in my skin.
But I'll win too,
for I will not cry.
What he will do is not to me.
His hand's a sucking fish on mine.
Our four feet jump over the broom.

## Supper

When I told him that was all the meat,
he said it was like my cheating self
to use up what belonged to him, then lie.
I was lower than a black widow spider
with an hourglass on her belly,
I was worse than white. His slurred hand
slung the kettle. The boiling soup
blanched my arms and face.
I took up the knife,
but he caught my wrist
as if it were a rabbit in
one of his traps, shook it,
broke its neck.
At my feet hot flies were buzzing
around the scattered bits of pig,
the splashed greens.

## *He is beginning to complain*

He is beginning to complain of pains
like sharp lights across the window that go and come.
When the stuck doll
rots in its grave under the dogwood,
he will die.
      It is a cheerful thing to kill weeds,
to slice their necks and hoe them down.
At noon I nurse the baby, knowing he will be
the last of Esau's blood. His little mouth sucks greedily
at my thin blue milk. I tell him soon child, soon.

## Cleaning Cotton at Night

Yesterday a black cat ran across my feet
and turned to white before he reached the wall.
Tonight the smooth cotton bolls prick
and scratch in the almost dark. The bowl
of seeds spills to the hot dirt.
Are there bayous where they sold you, Mama?
Has your new hair turned gold?
Do you eat white flour bread every day?
When will you send for me? No. Enough lies.
What do you think of your precious master now,
who could not stand the sight of you
so sold you south for a mule and a boy?
And what would you think of me, Mama,
growing into you, each day stranger
than the last. I am learning to sing
out of my hand, and the songs are terrible:
black girls in white with blood on their
foreheads, forced marriages to the cold worm.
And I know things.
That the morning glories will not close tonight.
That somewhere in Louisiana you will die
with a nail in your foot, and your jaw locked shut.

## Breaking Master's Leg

I broke master's leg with my song.
Because of me, he fell from his big, red horse.
Because I sang him down, sang
the bone through his skin.
                              When they found him,
he was trying to put it back
but the bald bone, being free, held on.
I was the crow who flew just then
into the certain clouds.
It was my tune the bone-egg sang
in its white sharp voice, humming
through the fingers of master's useless hands.

## Patsy Is Over

Now that I have withered to a quarter hand
they have sent me to the women's house.
Here I rock the unsold babies,
croon to the little ones that run
across the dirt floor, quick and blind as crabs.
At noon the mothers come,
and their heavy sweat fills the room
as they ease their nipples into parting mouths.
The children suck the sweet fooling milk.
Later, their smooth mothers gone,
they will remember who it is loves them most,
whose words they hear from their darkest sleeps
moaning to them, time on time, how it will be,
the day they rise in white to see
their multitudes, shining in the grass.

*from* ACROSS HER BROAD LAP
SOMETHING WONDERFUL
(1989)

# Things

A telephone is ringing in the field.
The cattle circle it,
wondering if it will feed them.
When they graze away,
they leave a ring of flat seed-heads
in the high wheat.

In the river, clothes are washing.
They rub against the rocks.
Sheets are weaving themselves
in and out of the current.
A red dress billows downstream.
A done shirt is spreading its sleeves
on a blueberry bush.

In the house, the kettle is boiling.
Little steamy breaths huff over
the stove 'til all the water's
gone. Then, slowly, the bottom
burns through. First red, then white,
then, through a rust-edged hole
the first blue flame inside.

## The Old Cat

One milky eye looks nowhere.
The other is dark.
All day long he miaows too loudly,
pacing the shed.
He climbs on the saw table.
When he tries to scratch
a hole in the heaped dust,
he hits wood.
It is not food he wants,
deep in his orange fur.
One taste, and the miaowing begins
again. You pick him up.
Your fingers find his bones.
He is smaller than he seems.
You were five when he crawled
onto our porch, his throat huge.
And since then, four times
his life has drained, red and white,
from some abcess. The last time,
you put your head down
on his deflated body on the cool
metal table, and sobbed. The papers
I would have signed are still waiting.

He is no different from any of us.
I remember Father, staring at the hospital wall
with his old eyes, and saying
I'm fed up with all these cloudy days.
When is the sun going to shine
as outside in the dark the stars flew.

*for D'Arcy*

## Loving a Son

hurts, like the stars
that are always there,
even in the day sky as if,
looking up, I could see them
past your lifetime and mine.
Do you remember the night
we showed the stars to Django?
He was three, and we held him
as he liked to be held
and we said, pointing up,
See, there's the Bear,
there's the Swan,
and it was his first time,
the first of all the Bears
and Saucepans made of light,
something for him to keep
as the fuzz deepens on
his lip and chin, and he goes
out alone nights, carrying
the car keys—a way to know,
looking up, what to look for,
and how it feels, held close,
when you find it.

*for Gerald*

# A Confluence

The clear Ichitucknee fingers into
the dark red Santa Fe,
which carries purity and great cold
downstream
until it is lost in murk of sun,
where wrist-thick moccasins ess along
and alligators surface, then disappear,
or drag their bellies up the muddy shore.
We have forgotten who we were,
young and eager, kissing through the
telephone. The Suwanee is in no hurry,
has rocked all the humming afternoon.
Now she takes two yarns from the basket
at her side, and with long white needles
begins to knit. The low sun glints
on the tips of her flying. Across her
broad lap, something wonderful begins.

# *from* FORTY-FOUR AMBITIONS
# FOR THE PIANO
# (1990)

## To Play Pianissimo

Does not mean silence,
the absence of moon in the day sky
for example.

Does not mean barely to speak,
the way a child's whisper
makes only warm air
on his mother's right ear.

To play pianissimo
is to carry sweet words
to the old woman in the last dark row
who cannot hear anything else,
and to lay them across her lap like a shawl.

## Staccato

The woodpecker drums
about the tree
a rising spiral

until even the highest smallest leaves
cannot help themselves

but shiver, then turn wild
at his bald beak
his head of stopped fire.

# Octave

It is what happens
when you spread the fingers of one hand.

It is the shadow
the bell's deep swing casts
on the desert, the round sound
of Ishi's mouth.

It is the sun
and her sister moon, slow-dancing.

It is what returns
when you are most alone,
calling across some dark orange dawn
to the farthest rim of rock.

## Accidentals

Driving Thirteenth Street, I have the sense that something has moved since yesterday. The avenues as usual count down to Main, yet when I arrive at work, I find the turn has taken me half a block to the north.

In the elevator I push three instead of four. I spend the rest of the day compensating, leaning slightly to the right to allow for the unexplained weight on my left shoulder.

*When the news came, we adjusted,* says the family of the man who will not come home tonight. *Yes,* puts in his wife. *We have schedules to keep.* But sometimes I slip, and cook for four. And sometimes, when I go to serve, I find the food has gone, and all my pots are full of tears.

# Grace Notes

Sometimes dance,
Astaire's clean brush before he taps.

Or beast,
the appetite surging in a hunter's throat.

Or flight,
a sail catching its breath before
it exhales the wind.

Sometimes lethal
brakes screaming before a car blooms.

Or lingering
the way a tongue tastes metal long after
the nail's rung home.

But always clairvoyant.
They know the stranger I will meet,
the trip I will take over water,
like Astaire,
whose last dance blossomed into air.

# True Legato

*Perfect seamlessness between notes can be achieved only
when the distance between them can be bridged without
changing the position of the hand.*

Lifting one foot, the other falls,
walking over grass where a child
sleeps, whose small stare closed
to dark. So these hundred years
become one more, and a boy's mother
touches his hair one day and sees
in his eyes that he is no longer
a child.
     And she reads the stone
which says, *Waking to Angels,*
and she tries to trace the notes back
whose stems break in her hands.
Lost, she rocks the tattered score.
She does not know she sings.

# The Prodigy

He was born with the fingerpads of the blind.
By eight he could tell if someone
had been at the piano before him,
and how long before, and who.
Beginning *Für Elise* one November afternoon,
he burst into storms of tears
because his sister had banged
her tuneless anger the night before,
and he felt the bruises still on the keys.

He was born with the ears of a dog.
He could hear his mother's skin decay,
the soft give
as her cheeks sagged just barely more.
Sometimes his face would cloud
because the moan of needles becoming
earth seemed so incomparably sad.
Or brighten. He had heard
the sun come out on the beating feathers
of birds, miles away.

He was born with his life in his hands.
Toddling, he learned the little bells
of Grieg. Then he mastered Mozart's
speech, its ache of clean and brittle
song. Then he learned to follow Bach,
crossing water from calm to flood,
up and down the steppingstones
of the keys. He would dream
of his piano as if it were flesh.
In a room with a strange instrument
he would walk by it once or twice
brushing it, as if by accident,
with his leg, his sleeve.

## Why Performers Wear Black

Because there is no black flower.
Because they are brides.
So that their hands can reach out of earth.
Because this is not practice.

Because they have agreed
not to talk with their mouths.
Because they know that sound
carries best at night,

the dip of feeding oars,
the loons' tremolo cry,
a whisper muffled in a woman's hair
on the far, dark shore.

# Fortissimo

To play fortissimo
hold something back.

It is what the father does not say
that turns the son.

The fact that the summit cannot be seen
that drives the climber on.

Consider the graceless ones:
the painter who adds one more brush stroke.

the poet of least resistance
who writes past the end of his poem.

# *Adagio*

The swing in the hips of a man
who's known the sea,

the dim roll and drag,
the black or turquoise water

on which he walks, on shore
or far from land.

There is the peace in him
of the bird

who begins her warble knowing
she has all day to sing.

# Ritardando

For months Gahagan gathered in
his heart

like chrysanthemums,
like onions that shine in jars.

And he leaned across the fence
and talked weather,

Miss Kappleman recalls,
the day he took three guns

and loops of bullets
and went downtown.

# Technique

Rock your hand
as though gentling a jar
where dark-chopped fruits have slept
among the lemon peels.

*My wrists turn easily in air*
*yet when I bring them to the keys,*
*they stiffen.* Of course.
Such freedom takes a life
of long and daily exercise

until finally
every muscle moves the hand
and your boat begins to slide
along the river
red with years of leaves.

Around a bend
there is a tin-roofed house
on algaed piers
in whose one room
a woman's wrist shines

as her hand moves
across the page. If you beached now
you could walk there in an hour.
But you will not,
having chosen to go by water.

## Sight-Reading

Halfway through, you realize
you know this room,

you know this glass of low gold,
you know the light that falls

on his hair, you know the eyes
of the Pole, Stefan,

how they feel on the skin
underneath your dress. And

you know the dim hall, how
you two lean on opposite walls,

how the air between you burns.
And you know you have beaten

the same circle, to return
to the place,

here in a stranger's house where
it seems forever ago

your sudden hands first told you
you were lost.

# The Uses of the Metronome

Before you get sea legs
    you place each foot like a drunk
        walking a line.

You are a darer of tightropes,
    each clenched inch
        braced for a fall.

But when the windy second comes
    thinking nothing,
        you balance to the deck's tilt


then, oh then, the world is utterly blue,
    the white sail slaps sky
        and you fly, you fly.

## The Power of the Right Foot

The power of the right foot
to hum the past
when the hand's moved on

is a high charge, not for
mirroring the scream
of the woman who cannot forget

anything, nor for ruining
clean whites by washing them
with something red.

Oh, the foot must never nod
asleep, but listen,
each toe listening, deep

in the quick of its nail
for the moment
the bride in her stitched pearls

turns to her groom
and smiles,
and lifts her veil.

# Some Members of the Chord Family

## The Major

Every morning he waxes his moustache
with a tiny brush, finishing the ends
with a curl between finger and thumb.
His mother never had to tell him
to sit up straight. Early on
he taught himself to deploy food
accurately to his high mouth
without looking down, a musical
skill akin to finding one's bedroom
door, no matter how dark the room.
At thirty he devised a six point
inspection scheme he has never
felt the need to change. Looking
into the mirror, he begins it now.

## Minor, His Wife

They met at Fort Meade the summer
of forty-two. She dove into the pool
in her new green suit. A strap broke.
For a moment, her white breasts
swung free.
            That night the Major sat
on the edge of his bed. She was
an advance on his map, a skirmish
to be won. Across the battlefield
of his dreams he moved his tanks,
his guns.
            Dry, her pale hair floated
around her face. Her eyes were
the changing shades of water.
In all their married life, he never
quite touched her.

## Diminished, Their Daughter

Amid the Dulles rush, she perches
on her case, with its remnants
of old destinations hanging from
limp strings. Her father has not
seen her fresh-dyed hair, nor
the shaven moon above her ear
which bristles to her palm.
For this, she shrinks to go home.
Yet, waiting, she is a quetzel
among crows, a flash of green
and crimson feathers. She has
arrived carefully early. There is
no chance she will miss her plane.

# *Modulation*

## *lone*

At five, with tight French braids,
I paraded to the teacher's clapping hands.
But when Easter came,
I alone refused to be a duck.

## *lean*

At fifteen, three fast inches
stretched my spine. Minutely
I'd examine each inch of flesh
during endless English, French,
and Art. To the assignment
*Tell me who you are,* I wrote,
"A pencil with pimples."

## *learn*

At thirty I discovered on a page
the themes of wind and stone.
And in my darkened house,
with its children sleeping
beyond the one lit lamp,
I lost my mirror's name.

## *lone*

And now at forty, having
fled California, I return.

I am a sharp-topped rock
off Point Reyes, the one
that makes a cave at low tide.
Every year I am less. One day
I will be air on your cheek,
a single grain of sand
over which each November
the black ducks will fly,
and the monarchs, with
their thousand paper wings.

# Fermata

Fermata the thin silk umbrella
that shelters the box

whose strings fall away.
Fermata the paper husk that falls

from the gift we can unroll
across the sky, though our dull

eyes cannot say how red moves
to orange, or yellow to blue.

Fermata the moon, the white
light that holds, the full woman

who watches without impatience
her own blossoming.

Fermata the oil made of light
which continues past its frame.

The rest of Lepic is here,
on the gallery wall. Oh see,

he has taken a step outside.
He is in my heart now,

as long as I live, like the woman
he hunts in every Paris street,

who came to him like a dark wind
from the south; the woman, Fermata.

# Playing Hiroshima

*There are no finer audiences in the world.*
—Ivo Pogorelich, *Pianists Speak.*

Did you know the ones with colds wear surgical masks
so as to disturb no one?
They do.

Did you know their small hands lie folded in their laps
like boats?
They do.

Did you know they kneel kimonoed for études, as tea
cooled by a mother's breath?
They do.

Did you know that skin can fall like snow?
Softly . . . . . . . pianissimo.
They do.

# The Pianist's Next Day

Someone else
walked from the wings last night

black tails
adangle like dead crows. I mourn now

that, desperate,
I turned to him. I wake the less

for putting on
the stranger's blasé eyes who bowed,

set his bench,
them embalmed, note perfect, each piece

I played.
See my knuckles whiten—the bald heads

of an audience
all in a row. Listen. The marks

on my face
are the burns of their applause.

# The Pianist Who Keeps a Loaded Gun on Her Piano When She Practices

The children know not to knock.
Double-sexed, I use both hands.
I tease seriously. The notes
tantalize, approach explosion,
fall back. It is the brink
that thrills when the high
walker sets her pink foot
on the rope.
            The children know
I would shoot, but not at whom.
I am not certain I know myself,
only that this deep readying,
this fierce first step over air,
is worth dying for.

# *from* HUNGER
## (1993)

---

# The Cow

Across her teeming back I strew
the poison cure.

Her tail turns still.
Soon she will be less thin.

But then again the black buzz,
the keen upheaving bone.

And though I glove my hands
I cannot help but breathe.

The sharp dust drifts,
each time deeper.

*Don't do it,* says my husband
who loves me, hearing

the hundred tiny cuts in
my throat. He does

not know how it feels
when the flies lift.

# Farm Wife

She tends the red geraniums.
When their clustered eyes go dark,
she cuts them from their stems.
With her thumb she strokes the
furry leaves, not like common cloth
but the nap and shift of velvet
falling heavy over her hips,
the long slow dance
of Paris, in France.
The swoony glide of his knife
spreading butter.
Not the bread it takes her
all day to bake,
the coarse knead and punch,
but the rise,
the pale cheek of flour,
the dip and shimmer of the heat,
the arched backs of the hills
in their arms of sky.

# Elegy

*Red-shouldered at four o'clock*
swings binoculars to the right
over the breast of the ridge
to zoom the lone bird
that screams, passing the cold
rocks of Hawk Mountain.
And a chill seeps into the pockets
of the watchers to climb,
as the light fails, higher.
You unscrew the wine. We drink
from the same skin and when
the call comes *Sharpies at eleven*
we swing our eyes south.
This is what we came for, Harry.
To become, only for a moment,
what we dreamed we were as children.
Something wild, flying away.

*for Harry Humes*

## At Eighty

Perhaps the white with the sewn pearls,
as evenly strung as la-las. Then again,
maybe the dark blue, whose double buttons
gleam. Or the shawl for a change,
with its hooked-in holes and metal glints
running through the yarn.
                                  She stands
at the closet, considering, as before
a late-night shop, whose lit displays
look like nothing she ever owned.
And suddenly the choice matters terribly.
Her spotted hands begin to shake.
She is so afraid to be wrong.

# The Dresser

For months no one has opened a drawer
and inside
the tight-legged piles of underwear
the rolled-together socks that hate each other,
the shirts with their sleeves crossed
behind.

The oak grain has begun to swell
as a can will, whose red insides
have not been boiled past memory.
*But these are only clothes.*
*Familiar things.*
*You dramatize.*
        No.
When they opened the mouth
of the cave
where the boy king slept in gold,
it was the simple air that screamed.

# The Laws of Women

The blood mouse hangs by her tail
and dropped, whirls down.
What returns is so clear
you could drink it.
Children sometimes do. And dogs.
But not us. We have rules
for what we drink.
And when we wake in the barking night
we have learned
to flush, not thinking,
what has seeped most darkly from ourselves.

# Flood

*Alexandria, Louisiana*

We have been four days on the second floor.
Four days since the brown water first
entered our home. It is two steps up,
and rising. Roberta holds my hand.
Her small fingers frighten, even in
my palm. Her braids pale around her face.
*Hush,* I tell her. *Can you hear it?*
And when she stills, we hear it.
Not with our ears
but with the parts of our bodies that know.
With our knees, with our low places.
Snakes, swimming.

# On Passing Forty

You with your mesmerizing eyes,
you holding a daubed cracker
between first finger and thumb,
so absurd in your huge foreign hands.
You the priest, with your obscene thoughts.
The gold water in your glass disappears,
leaving ice. And you look up.
I will not go with you.
I am happy. I have decided
my life, and it does not take place
in rooms like these.
                        In certain years
marriage darkens in my throat.
In certain years I am aware
of the way white hairs fall
around my face, killing the black ones
underneath. I smile too much,
and the skin deepens around my mouth.
At times like these you appear.
In the street you pause to buy a paper,
and your eyes travel my body
leaving it throbbing,
bright and pulpy as a heart.
At a party, as now, you single me,
and my fingertips shiver as though
I'd run them around your white collar,
pulled it wide, set my lips to your
bare skin. *I am happy,* I say.
The wind gathers your black cape,
and sends it flying.

# For Someone Considering Death

I told you.
Life is one big Hanon
up and down the piano,
ten fingers skipping over each other
in every conceivable way,
two hands getting stronger.

And sure,
the notes are the same for everyone,
but you can choose to whisper or shout,
to fade or grow.
And haven't you noticed that some people's hands sing,
but others are Midwestern on the keys,
each crescendo a secretarial swell.

Think about this.
How can you dream to play the *Pathétique*,
how can the moment come to truly look
into someone's eyes
and say, *The hell with everything, I love you,*
when you haven't done your time,
hour after hour, year after year
in that small closed room.

# Six Cairns for Mary

*Where the way over the moors turns indistinct, heaps of stones serve to guide the walker along the authorized path. No one alive remembers who dragged them there.*

## Mary Attends a Ball (1830)

Our candles shine plain as servant girls
before the moon, who wears the whitest dress
tonight. And all our India muslins,
and all our fine combs of filigree,
and all our long feathers
cannot rival how she flies.
And when the gentlemen roam the hall
there comes a moment each forgets
the face or name of her he seeks.
And when memory returns, each thinks
himself wrong, it was someone else
he hunted, with such white fever.

## Mary in Love (1832)

If Mr. Peake stands booted on Ingleton Hill
and his big mare stamps beside him
whose rein's a hard dry catch in his palm,
and if the day spreads her fields,
yellow as head powders at his feet,
and he is thinking which are ripe
and which not, then I would go to him
in the little wind which stirs his hair
and creeps among the folds of his stock
just before, all around,
the gold seed wisps begin to sway.

## Mary, Waking (1833)

*Well, Mrs. Peake,* he says. And smiles.
And when he's shut the door I rise
and put on my new dress, habit of wife,
gray as the feathers of doves
that peck at the bright litters
of corn someone strews for them
by the barn, whose stones weigh
heavier than hearts, more
than any man can heft alone.

## His Breakfast Plate: The Litter of Mr. Peake (1835)

Yellow smears upon a white ground.
Two greasy commas that remain of chops.
A knife thrust through the fork's tines.
And, over all, the scattered dots of crumbs
brushed from his hands as,
pig-shine on his lips, he turns to go.

## Mary's Duties (1836)

He is rid away to the tenant farms
and I take up my pen to list
the shakings-out and openings.
And my thin letters lean as sails
that, though driven, cannot arrive.

*May the ninth,* I write.
And: *Mrs. Ferguson.*
*Unbutton the bed pillows*
*and plump them to the air.*
Then: *Take the curtains down*
*and with your broom unseat*
*the spiders' webs. Open*

*the windows and leave them*
*wide* and here the thread trails
off, among the cottages
with their spring festoons of eggs
pricked with pins and blown,
fragile as the blacksmith's daughter
dreaming in the sun, who lifts
her skirts above her white knees.

I pull back behind a hedge.
Let her not meet me, with my dry pen.

## The Very Reverend Charles Easton (1836)

Thursday last Mary Peake fell off her horse
and lit upon her ear.
She never spoke again, died in half an hour,
the child still in her.

This night the cat got to her corps,
et off bits of her nose and chin.
The rest took wind,
and is now in all our mouths.

# The First Dinner Party—The Puzzles of the Meal

Among the forest of forks and spoons
the young girl need not fear
who remembers that, as with life,
the proper meal progresses from outer,
to inner, settings. In conversation
with a partner, etiquette demands she not
assault his ear with girlish questions:
Don't you just adore Wagner? What are your
*favorite plays?* until the gentleman
has satisfied his appetite, and then
she must speak only softly, and seldom,
on topics proper to her femininity.
When the finger bowl arrives, she must not
wash her grapes. If doubtful of the ways
of oranges, she must choose bananas.
When standing to leave the table, a lady
does not fold her napkin at her plate
but lets it fall, as too careful placement
implies an unseemly intention to return.

Oh Myrtle, do you think such rules
can truly bind the darker dinners of the heart?
As Charles is your brother, do you believe
I can win his favor laughing only gently,
speaking seldom, or might I, reaching across
the table, all the servants sent upstairs,
tell him quickly how I yearn? Might I wash
his grapes and hand them to him one by one?
If I, saying nothing, leave my napkin
folded by his plate, will he understand?

# Sweet Pea Embroidery in Rose and Heliotrope

Let the needlewoman gather
a handful of the blossoms she loves most.
Now let her embroider in silks
the colors of that scent that entered
her room, its wilds of heliotrope, of rose.
But let her tell no one
how she left her bed, to stand
in her white nightgown among flowers.
And how the knowledge came to her
of what she can, and cannot, own.

# How to Cut and Dry: Study of a Marriage

*With care the hedgerows can provide a thrifty wife with
winter bloom. Most prized of all is Honesty, which must not
be cut until quite dry, and should then be hung upside down
until its seed pods can be removed, leaving only the white
discs within.*

It is so cold these days that my fingers stiffen,
reaching into the privet. This morning,
I cut my wrist on some brambles
but did not notice until the blood ran.
I have filled the house with winter's gifts.
In every closet something lies stiffening
between layers of old news. I have just
replaced the milkweed pods that used to stand
in a copper jug by the front door. They had
exploded, spilling seed across the entry. He
will not notice the fresh green limbs of pine.

# Cookery: To Truss Small Birds

*Thread wheatears, ruffs, or quails on a long skewer, four or more together. Pass the skewer through the wingtip of each bird, and out its body to the next. Secure with string.*

See the little birds on their burning branch.
Their song sizzles from their beaks.
Their wings are tied.
How they would fly otherwise, on this ecstatic wind!

# Secrets of the Fur Trade

Sable is for ladies of quality. The best
is Russian, with fine white hairs running
through the dark. They will try to sell you
poorer stuff, with badger hair glued in,
but you need not be fooled. Blow through
the fur. You will see the stiff lies,
which do not easily yield to a lady's
breath. Watch the merchant's eyes narrow,
as he sees you understand. If you'd asked
for rabbit, he'd have brought you cat.
Now tell him that you know, as well
as you know your own name—Esmée—
the greenish color of wet dyed fur,
the dark brown of the true. That he
must bring you from the back room
where his wild son sits, ruining
his brown eyes over poems
(in which dim animals cross the snow
to be finished, one by one, for
the white moments of their coats)
the long fur of all their lives.
That you will purchase only this from him:
this rare darkness tipped with light,
to clothe your body in, against the many winters
a lady of quality must endure.

# Fashion: How to Wear the Veil

With black jet stars artfully placed
above a bare chin. This is the way
of the flirt. With the veil caught
back, to hang unhampered to the wearer's
waist. This is the way of the free
American, of the summer girl.
Then, there is the decorous way,
the understatement from a hat.
This is the way of the well bred.

And finally, there is the nun,
who goes differently veiled, morning
and afternoon. This is the way of
the truly passionate, the way of
the woman who stands in the wind
at the needle's shiny point, her
face covered, who does not look down.

# from *Exteriors, a Self-Guided Tour*

## *Room 1 (Mexico, Oils 1969–71)*

*Avenida*

Here is the street, the way the heat
settles in the dust.
If it rained now, the first surge
would be lost, would puddle then
hurry up and dry as though it never came,
the way the bride does not remember
her wedding night, how her new man
unzipped black legs. She has forgotten
the strange dripping weight
like the oppression of withheld rain.
She looks out the window.
                              One thin child
hops in the avenue. Over a dust line
into a little cloud, and back again.
He keeps his arms tucked to his sides
and she thinks of the thousands
of small singers at home, jittering among
the crowded leaves.
                         They came to the capitol
for Juan's work. All day he hammers copper
into suns. When he comes from the market
the din comes too, clings to the folds
of his shirt, lingers in his fine
cheek hair. She turns warm tortillas
into a basket. He pulls her around.
There is a hint of metal on his tongue
as though he had licked money.
                                   You can

just see her face at the edge of the third
window. She has hung a blanket over the hole
to keep out the dust. I never intended
to paint her. I wanted only the street,
the child with the dry mouth.
I meant all the windows to be dark.


*Fábrica*


I choose a brush to make the thick
streak of the sun behind the factory.
Juan is leaving. I steal the jacket
from his shoulders, and its umber
migrates to the smokestack
and fades into the air.
                              Pepe pays
no attention. He has a woman
to get to who wears a print dress
and high heels, and can cook arroz
like no one in this world.
He is the one I want.
I have put on his face
what he feels, entering her door.

# Room 2 (Mexico, Watercolours 1972–73)

*View of Dzibilchaltún*

I make my softest brushes from the hairs
of my own head. Only these understand
to wash so faintly
that the shadow hand which cups
a cheek can be rendered private,
safe from those who look,
then go.
      There is a sky in my
*View of Dzibilchaltún* that recalls
the slow violet light of bruises.
For this and for the river, I used
such brushes. They sold none there,
and my case held nothing so lost.
So I tied my own pulled hairs
and from their tips water began
to flow over my stippled paper,
burying the false starts underneath,
the jumbled heads, the botched bones,
heaped so high the ferry sometimes
scrapes, and the boatman swears to
the Virgin between rotting teeth
until his pole catches deeper,
and his flat boat slides on. She
was not with me then. I sat alone
on the damp grass, finishing the water,
beginning to wash in the sky.
And I put into the picture what
I did not paint, the fading pastel
houses of the rich who do not come
from Veracruz any more, the unglazed
pots of the poor, who sling their
hammocks in the big rooms, the bird eyes
of the old woman who killed

her one chicken for a guest then
gummed the claws, refusing more,
while he, I, ate all the rest.
                    You say,
*these are not there?* She found them.
She looked into the river
then turned silent, staring across
the London dark, through the rain.

# Room 3 (London, Various Media 1974–79)

*Night Cove* (Watercolour)

I scrape the thin line
off a shrimp's back
and clean my knife on paper
which, opened, explodes with
star–bursts of entrails.
There is a pile of heads and shells.
There is a heap of boneless embryos.
Shrimp curl inwards, like her asleep.
She is so pale the veins shine
in her breasts. Her hair spreads
faint strands, like feelers, over
the pillow. Her lids are ghost eyes,
like the eyes of cave fish
who do not need light. I think
she would gleam in the moon
like something swimming.
                          I have
painted her like this. She is
the white glow that hovers under
the little boat in the night cove
where a father has taken his son
to fish, these two who go so that
the father can touch
the boy's shoulder in a way
he cannot, unless they are alone,
and the boy can understand
how he is loved. The moon
is making them a path over the
dark water. She is the pale streak
they do not see, finning past
their unbaited hooks as a woman
shifts in sleep, with this grace.

## Nude (pencil)

She leans nude into the Chelsea night.
There are no stars or moon,
only the wet splash of street lamps
and the glowing bars of zebra crossings.
I have put out the lights.
I am drawing her by feel, the arch
of one leg as she settles into
the window seat, like a white neck rising
from the Ness. Earlier, we tried
another kind of love. We thrashed
and surged in the sheets. I could not
reach her. She turned away,
the sad damp trailing along
her thighs.
      I am drawing her in the
dark, because if I see what my hand
is making I will never finish.
I will never again lie all night
by the lake, staring into its
black waters with such craving.

# from *Xtofer and Elizabeth*

## 1712: *He comes to the house*

He comes to the house and asks
How do ye, then looks out the window
at the fine clouds or the rainy weather,
then again at me as though I would answer
for it all. And then he smiles.
Then Father's from his walk, sets his thumbstick
in the stand, takes Xtofer's arm
and off they go, to the deep seats where men
discuss together, Father and his solicitor,
this very Christian lawyer.
And I, wondering what he means.

Times at night, when the coals
are red eyes in the ash
and the chambermaid is gone away,
I see Grandmother
when she was Jennet the child,
leaning on the stone sill
in the moon, her hair loosed yellow,
thinking for the first time
how very many stars there be.

# 1715: They have held the Assize of Bread

They have held the Assize of Bread
at Leeds, and set new rates
for wheaten loaves which enrage
the millers, says Xtofer,
and he and Father go on anent
the wet year, and the winnowing
of hay to fatten the barns
by Michaelmas if the stacks
be not rotten from beneath.
They do not glance at me,
and for my part I am sensible only
of the stuff that lies against
my skin. The chance brush of
petticoat along my unclothed leg
must drive me wild I think,
as our puss went that found
a small green herb, which he
rubbed at and purred deeper
in his throat than ever
I heard him do before. Then
he thought to bite its heart.
And went leaping through the grounds.
I can still conjure him, rolling
on the grass, huge dragon wings
ashiver in his mouth.

## 1716: The maids have carried off the mutton

*To X*

The maids have carried off the mutton
and pyes and we three nest in the parlour,
you and Father in your Virginia cloud, I
pricking out a pansy scheme, then beginning
to stitch it in. And here's sweet discussion
of some small matter, say the arrival of
a Doctor of Teeth in Bingley, Tuesday last.

And at this moment I am aware that my waist
presses against my gown. And I watch
your dear face in candlelight and consider
the story I'll tell when the bedcurtains
are drawn tonight.
           I have seen the grass
moving in just such a slight way
before the grouse break free, whose wings
beat high and sound like rain. I have
not caused their flight, but only
point it out. Think upon it if you will.
I am, dear Cedar, your most humble
and creeping bramble, Elizabeth.

## 1720: Elizabeth Danby I am

Elizabeth Danby I am, who was Wren,
and once more low with child.
She will be Jennet if she lives.
Never did I hear her sisters cry
but they lay ivoried in their white gowns.
When the last was dead he could not wait
the gander moon, but entered early,
with drawn tool. And shining eyes
like night sonnes. And now he writes
his name for two: *Xtofer.*

## 1723: The comfort is damp to the skin

The comfort is damp to the skin,
red satin like cold stone.
And I know Xtofer where you lye
though you think me a fool
who believes your mincing pleadings,
your words fine as dark thread
wet with her lips.
         I dreamt
you rode the stang, that they stuffed
you full of straw and stitched you up
and painted you crooked, catchpaper
varlet that snatches more than
your own, and on a stick you went
who were so dear to me, between
Cuddy the butcher, and Tom who
sells ale. And the smelly crowds
jeered you out and dogs ran after.
I wake to rain, and chill unseasonable,
and damp's frog mouth pressed to my bone.
In the next room you are dressing,
fumblefingers for the dark.
Outside stirs restless your stoned mare.
You cannot wait 'til morning, to go to her.

## 1724: Jennet stirs in so frail sleep

Jennet stirs in so frail sleep.
I stroke her three years curls,
more pale than they seem by day.
I hear he rode from the Angel
to the Two Necked Swan. He was
not alone, and will he return
I know no more than I know
of that place where kings' flesh
be venison and the true angels
weep and sing. I will stay
all night by her,
only to see her eyelids flutter.

Dearest Jennet, take my life,
this broken odd rhapsody of scraps,
and know the truth of love:
that no matter where you hide,
chyld or woman, the moon and stars
will cross the dark to find you.

# NEW POEMS

# Sleep Positions

This is how we sleep:
On our backs, with pillows covering our chests, heavy as dirt
On our sides, like wistful spoons
Clenched, knees in-tucked, arms folded
Wide, like sprawling-rooted lotuses.

In Iowa on pictures of Hawaii, huge white flowers on blue
In New York on black satin
In China on straw.

This is how our dreams arrive:
As hot yellow taxicabs
As sudden blazing steam, we who have been pots on a stove,
looking only at our own lids
As uninvited insects, all at once on our tongues.

O hairdresser, auditor, hard-knuckled puller of crab traps, you who
think poetry was school, you who believe you never had
a flying thought,
lie down.

# Grass

*San Antonio, Florida*

They don't mow on Sundays in San Antonio.
They keep the seventh day for Paz
and Neruda, for Simic angels
whose wings are made of smoke.

And they walk their dogs softly in
the mornings, so they will not miss
the smallest utterance of Whitman
or of John Clare, who pace the parks

early, when a ground fog's rising
and the oranges are lanterns
on their stems. And sometimes
they go to bed changed. And

they'll swear it was not they who
fumbled in their sheets at dawn,
as the poets rose like grass, and
the mowers coughed and were still.

# Eight Short Pieces

## Epitaph for a Poet

Here lies Richard.
He tried to improve on silence.

*for Richard Gormley Eberhart*

## The Teacher

The blackboard swirls with nebulae.
Someone before her
has written the truth there.
And erased it.

## Youth

A bright band circles your wrist
because it has fallen off your hair
which, slippery as black water,
would not be stayed.

*for a student, sitting under a noon tree*

## Crying

The baby cannot tell you what he wants,
so he wants it louder,
like a teenager booming rap down the street.


## Love

She tries it on, like a dress.
She decides it doesn't fit
and starts to take it off.
Her skin comes, too.


## Love and Cancer

Think small, the way ants
build their hills, a grain
at a time. If I could be
one cell in you, how ardently
I'd multiply. Until I was a hundred,
a million cells. Until I filled
so much of your X-rayed self
that if they cut me out,
you could not survive.

## Longing

A rich man comes to you.
And he is a good man.
And he kneels at your feet
And he says, *Tell me what*
*I can do to make you happy.*
But you can't answer him.
You can't answer him at all.

## Lillian

The men lean forward, all happy eyes,
as the young woman tells stories of herself.
She knows her stories charm,
but she does not know their charm will fade.
And that is what makes her so beautiful.

# You're Dreaming

Oh, you're dreaming all right, gold-rimmed and high-tired, slick around the curves as oiled hair, ten, a hundred, a thousand miles farther into the dark than you were.

Oh, you're dreaming all right, and your dream had dark brown gold eyes, and you thought of cats and claws, and you thought you'd burn if you didn't die first, and you're trying as hard as you can to blur to a metal streak.

Oh, you're dreaming all right, and you're gold as an angel yourself, with your Botticelli curls and your small hands, and I'm watching you sleep and I'm older than you, but I know that dream, to fly until you die of flying.

This is what it means, I tell you, in the deepest female parts of our dreams—comets, burning, ecstasy, nothing at all.

*for Lori*

# Love Story

*And what was the mountain Yaeko painted?*
*It was the voice of the air.*

And she painted it with oils whose faint cloud blue
stayed on her hands at night.

She would tie up her hair first, as if a wind were coming
as it did the day their group

made its way up Mount Miwa, and the wind
crossed her face with black feathers

as if something were shaking out of her, to reappear
calmly on the pond far below.

*And what was the mountain Yaeko painted?*
*It was the glow that remains when all*
*the other lights have dimmed.*

And she painted it for Hiroshi because he would not remember
how she looked that autumn afternoon,

when he said, seeing her alone,
Why don't you walk up with us?
because he would not remember

how, as they climbed the steep path, her hair came loose, and
flew across her face.

*And what was the mountain Yaeko painted?*
*It was the skein of the sea.*

And she sat on the cold train all day with the painting in her lap.
Finally, in the Tokyo dark, she arrived.

There is a character in Japanese whose radical is silk, and it means the deepest love a woman can have for a man.

It means connection, as by unbreakable thread, and its meaning does not admit bodily touch.

And it ends at the pointed tip of the brush, the wet gray finish of the character, as the hand falls to rest.

# Pastoral

The egrets like whitecaps on the plowed fields
The treeline across the long way arched
as a blanket over a sleeper's hip,
and over the road, the bahia where the cattle feed

And the pale moon, still there because she cannot
bear to leave the soft slope of the pond
where they sat as the man's fingers moved lightly
across her wrist, although he has turned and walked
away, and is even now thinking of someone else, the sun,
more beautiful in her flame clothes.

And the pond itself, where desire's secret fish swim,
their spread tails swaying in the shadowed light
as now, under the clodded earth of fields something
stirs as if stroked and seeds open, release

and easily, and this is how it is and no one is thinking
of the young woman in the blue print dress,
how one leg twisted under her and her mouth turned
red as he slammed her against the wall, desiring her
more than he has ever wanted anything and they fell
together on the unmade bed, she tearing at his clothes,
and this was opening too.

# The Dream Penitentiary

At first light, she rises from her cot
and gropes across the six feet of floor
towards what she thinks is a window
which every morning is still blank brick.
Then she turns inward and lifts from
beneath her thin mattress the letter
she has written in the night.
Her husband is there, disguised
as a guard. She hears him pacing
the echoing halls. He kneels
outside her cell, takes each word
from her, presses it to his heart.

# The Composer Interviews Her Piece

When presenting your plate for mashed potatoes
did you say, *Oh yes, PLEASE,*
to the spoon heaped high with snow?

When the moon was a grin in the black sky
and all the stars were clear,
could you rock it, just slightly, with your eyes,
and did it become a boat?

When Miss Heidemann said, *Now open* The Commentaries
*to page five,* could you get it out of your mind
how her white hair was flying from her skull,
and how her first name was Claire?

Could you follow instructions without coloring in the *o*s?
When you were very small, did you fight sleep?
Have you ever stopped fighting sleep?

# Appoggiatura and Fermata

Fermata, the older sister, envies
Appoggiatura's easy grace, covets
the way she slides downstairs
on silvery heels. Appoggiatura

teases Dad until he beams, changes
into honey for Mom. Alone, she
wanders room to room. She is real
only in the mirror of someone's face.

Fermata can stay quite still while
the last curve of sun flashes
green at the edge of the sea.
Whatever she is, she is forever.

# Composition

*Towards the end, his left hand became paralyzed, and during that period he wrote a beautiful piece for the left hand alone.*
                    —Mrs. Frederick Converse

It sings clearest which is nearest sleep.
The halfway child, humming to himself.
The old woman, thinned to a piano string,
who remembers suddenly the flash of green
she saw when she was six, and not again.
Of the remaining hands the right dances
in the air. The left holds still.

This is a piece for the left hand.

# Daddy's Writing

*One of the side effects of Parkinson's disease is the*
*progressive diminution of the size of the affected person's*
*handwriting.*

His alphabet shrinks until it is so tiny
it needs a magnifying glass.
The words are trying to vanish

but his twisted stubborn fingers
grip the pen's shaft, turn ink
in ever-smaller circles, the way

vultures close, vital, fearsomely
accurate, over something we cannot see
in the green and swaying field

## Dogwood, December

We notice not going but absence.
And therefore, looking through
the window at the framed tree,
for the first time we see its bones

and understand that the night
brought flurries, which lie
now on busy ground, out of
our line of view. And we think

how gray it is, how even the air
in the house seems gray. But
then we sense vibrations not quite
flutters, and a bunting, dazzling

as lazuli, appears, and another;
and then a canary in shy gold,
three cardinals, and a tiny
woodpecker, black and white,

with a crest bright as the tip
of a child's nose, who pecks
at the berries from underneath.
William Henry Hudson wrote

that the sky is always full of wings
but we do not see them unless
there is a storm. I used to think this
poetic, but untrue. I believe it now.

*for Peter Behr 1915–1997*

# For Mother, After the Vision Fire

*Point Reyes, California*

It is what you secretly thought, lying in bed at night.
That when you die, your particulars will disappear.
The kitchen where you held the coffeepot under
the faucet every morning at seven-ten exactly,
the frayed arms of the couches you had not replaced
because you were nearing your own death.
Instead, it all went first.

                The nutmeg wreath, the crèche,
the Christmas bells. The tall shelves of books you'd
have read if you had not run out of time. The painting
of the boy lying on his dreamy back that Daddy gave
you with such ceremony one birthday, having hidden
it for weeks in the garage. A list of losses to dry up
your pen. You were not there as witness. That was
no surprise.

             But how obscene it is, you here now,
poking at the warm ground, disturbing only ash that
puffs in soft gray clouds around the tennis shoes you
always wear. Like some human part, projecting hard
from the detritus of your burnt life, that you see
and do not want to name.

# The .38

The first time you unlocked your glove compartment and showed me
your secret, I was breathless at what nestled in its box like jewelry.
Then, slowly, I grew used to what rode with us, and on clear days,

when we'd drive to the beach, I came to understand it preferred
its double dark to our light, where you were touching my breasts
under my shirt. And as we began to think more and more about

our natures (you saw me as glitter flaked off schist; to me you were
the gesso angel that brought the annunciation), I decided I was not
sorry you kept it in your car, just there, not for anything. Until

the March afternoon you took it out, laid it across your hand,
and said, *Have I told you I have bullets?* Then the .38 turned rattler
across my path, and jealousy crept into me and I wanted it gone.

So you put it away, and it went back to sleep. And one midnight,
as we were heading home, south on 101, lights all around us, as if
we had been sent to the sky, I felt my nipple diminish as it

tightened, and I thought, because this was my first time, *Yes,
I will marry you.* But I didn't say it. So you had to pull up to
my parents' house in your red Mercedes that summer evening

and demand, *Come now.* But my parents and I were leaving.
You drove off, washed in the scent of gardenias at the top of
our garden. The rest of this is for the .38, because even

your ashes are forty now, and I don't think you're listening.
I'm sorry, .38. I was wrong. It wasn't you he craved after all.
It was the featherless bird he became when he stepped off the rail.

And all the way down to the steel water, he must have been happy
as he never was. Oh, .38, he has left us both. You were his sister,
his mother, his charm. You kept him safe as long as you could.

*for H. P.*

# Anger: Five Plays

### i

A swirling black rose of cloud
sends down a surgical light.
Aha! You're transparent!
Then you're opaque but
there's a stone on your tongue
which you can touch every day.

### ii

He conceals something
as he strokes her hair
with the backs of his fingers.
If he holds the something
differently, he can puncture
her. There are moments
he craves that hiss.

### iii

Anger sends cells moving, like refugees in long lines of cars.
The women in their kerchiefs stare dully out.
And when the cells arrive, they must fight for bread,
slap each other from the way,
then hunch over the hard loaves as if they were pregnant with them
and scuttle off alone, tearing and stuffing
with hands bruised from being first.

## iv

In retreat, not–things float like fish on their sides.
They have a white haze around their bodies
because they are already ghosts.
You flush them away. They are dirt, and that is
what you do with dirt.

## v

A hot spoon will burn a little moon scar on your lip.
You heat your food until the oven flames.
You get into the car and drive.
Tumbleweeds drift across your path, like women
throwing themselves under their husbands' wheels.
If you were on the coast, the blank cement
of water below the bridge
would be the most beautiful thing in the world.

# Night Waking

It's the moon, cooing like a dove in the barn.
Or the stars, scattered like handfuls of grain.
I will get up, sweep them off the black stone.
But *Hush* and *Hush* and *Hush*, says the night,
lapping at my shore. And more and more
I'm drawn, to walk the long cove, away
from this farm, these dry and beautiful hills.

# Times

The parking lots of K-Mart are not safe. There are video cameras on school buses, and metal detectors in the halls of universities. Every time she gives an F she feels something burn into the back of her neck.

When the telephone rings again at three A.M. with breathing and you startle awake, you know the police can do nothing, unless afterwards. The chain rattling at your entry cannot kill you. So you tell yourself, as you dial 911, the believer's number.

Elsewhere, food sent to starving Somalis is sold in little heaps on the street: rice, flour, the dry powder that is milk. In Bosnia, children are born already raped. Their mothers do not know any more what to love.

There is a man held in the dark. He is not allowed to speak. One day, the chatter of the guards, record played backwards, fades out. At the man's door a poem softly knocks. He memorizes it. The poem is his charm, his small control. It is how he stays alive.

# Dearborn North Apartments

*Chicago, Illinois*

Rows of rectangles rise, set into brick.
And in every rectangle, there is a lamp.
Why should there be a lamp in every window?
Because in all this wide city, there is not
enough light. Because the young in the world
are crazy for light and the old are afraid
it will leave them. Because whoever you are,
if you come home late but it looks like noon,
you won't tense at the click as you walk in
which is probably only the heat coming on
or the floorboards settling. So when you
fling your coat to its peg in the hall, kick
off your heels, unzip your black velvet
at that odd vee'd angle as if someone
were twisting your arm from behind,
then reach inside the closet for a hanger,
just to the dark left where the dresses live,
what happens next is a complete surprise.

# *Words*

Some hang in the air like diesel fumes.
Some spread with the scent of
flowering vines, so a child, playing in
a cross-town park lifts her head,
and wonders what is about to happen.
Some arrive in flocks, to chitter side
by side on wires which vibrate
with their weight, like plucked strings.
Others camp wherever they can find
on the hard white winter of the page.
Growing cold and colder, they dig
into the snow. They hold each other,
say out loud what would have been
too large, too foolish. Night falls.
In the morning the page is blank again.

# How Do You Reconcile Teaching Computer Science with Being a Poet?

Either way, my hands move across the keys
even in the dark.
Either way, my fingers are not themselves,
tapping those little drums.

It is easy to love words the way zero loves one,
easy to take the sound that parts
the middle of the night
the way a boat's prow parts the sea—

*was it an owl?*
*was it a mouse?—feeling something sharp lift its fur*
*and then it's flying*

—and multiply it:
a blurred ring round the moon
the tossed rock of a man's heart,
as a woman lifts her bare arm.

A program calls across the gulf, just at dusk,
when the sun is the rose of a bird's egg,
and the subprogram replies.
She does not say what he thought she would.
He thought he knew her.
But no.

And you're sailing without your Loran, which is blinking
incessantly, like someone startled by light
or someone trying all constellations at once.
And you surge hard against the black water,
dragging a trail of stars.
Steer now. Steer safe. Steer for the cooling towers
that rise like a city across the swells.

# The Maker of Lines

## i. How I Became an Engineer

When I was little, they gave me dot to dots
with black points scattered like stars in reverse.
But they made a mistake: they numbered the stars.
I saw the elephant they wanted me to see. I saw
the dog. I saw the igloo, the fur round the Eskimo's
floating smile. *Why bother,* I said.
                                    But then one day
(I was five), I tucked my tongue between my teeth
and I blacked the numbers out. Then I pressed hard
between the dots, with lines so strong they veed
the page. My mother said the pictures looked like
nothing. Not to me. They looked like lines.
And I made them. And they could not be erased.

## ii. The Seed Road

> In order to generate support for the first cross-country
> highway, stretches of roads were improved in rural communities
> to show the public how comfortable travel could be.

We poured a batter of rock and sand.
We wet the slowly setting slabs, worked
them smooth with 2x4s, laid them
end to end like truths set down, over
the rutted tracks the locals called road.
And all at once their bones stopped
jittering. Their throats cleared of dust.
They were like anyone who has lived long
with pain. They did not understand
how hard they'd braced, until they felt

their shoulders loosen, as if something
warm were unfolding inside, yawning,
stretching sleepy wings.


### iii. The Engineers Hear from the Public

We divided the land in squares and looked
at the map through them, the way our wives
might look through their veils at church. And
we listened in a row of suits, as one by one
you approached the microphone. And
as you spoke, we drew a sprawl of lines,
like fishing net spread on hills and plains.
We gave you what you asked. You wanted
to be somewhere else, and soon. But let me
make this clear. We never said you were
anything but fish. We never promised things
would be different when you arrived.


### iv. Highways

Highways crack with weather and are not repaired.
Their bridges moan, as the slow damp gnaws
them red. Where are the young engineers,
their starched sleeves pushed to the elbows,
the curled black hairs on their forearms electric?
In the light of day
                    the salesman in his battered
Ford, trunk crammed with samples, fresh
shirts on a rod in the back seat, must cross
broken glass when he turns into the new city,
past the airport where each jet's roar comes
to nothing in the blue air.

# She Drives

She's driving    Past cheap flashes of motels    past
the off-price shopping malls where she doesn't pause
because she knows she can never spend enough
the way she knows that there aren't roads enough but
that's different and she still dreams to travel every one
until she passes every house with a light left on
every upstairs where a mother lies awake at three
then four for the son who said he'd be home early tonight
every gas station where a boy hoses rainbows away
every on-ramp where a stubbled hitcher squats
looking like someone escaped    every treeless street
of crewcut lawns where clouds of twelve year olds
buzz after school    where someone knifed a kitten
and stuffed it in a wall    She wants to pass by every house
where people have blossomed beyond themselves
She likes interstates because they blur    but
she likes the dirt roads too where they've sold
the pines for pulp and abandoned what was left
to creeping ferns    She likes the live-oaked streets
of Oxford Mississippi likes the midwest for the courage
of its corn    likes Maine for its dissolving rocks along
the coast    She'll tell you the subject is roads    the dips
the potholes the cliffs the curves the blasted-out interstates
that make liars of mountains    But somewhere there's
a long car with hooded lights looking to pull in her drive
She thinks if she doesn't stop moving    she can't be found.

# Interstate Dreams

*When the first 126 miles of Pennsylvania interstate were opened in 1940, postcards were printed with airbrushed moons and the potholes airbrushed out, thereby making the perfect road.*

And why not? It's smooth traveling we want, why pretend otherwise? And here's a night thought. When we set off for Newfoundland, is it the fjord at Gros Morn that grabs our breath or the road under us, the way we can think it goes on forever?

Do old highways have afterlives? Is there somewhere a glowing 301 lined with neon the way satin lines a skirt, an eternal 301 whose motels shine with finny cars outside each room, whose swimming pools teem with little boys and their shy sisters in new one-piece suits?

At certain stretches are there not ghosts? The headless girl who drove a wild Mercedes under a truck? The nurse, who flew white-capped for a moment across the on-ramp as her car door flapped like a mouth that keeps saying, uh uh uh? Or the man who swayed into six lanes of traffic one black night as if he were dancing, and met the lights in the second lane?

And why should freeways not slide between cities like great fish while lines of cars and semis and helmetless cyclists sit on their backs? Why do you believe this is not true? Because your parents told you it is you who move? What did you expect them to say?

What is a pothole after all but a place where the earth protests, where it shifts and shifts again, until it shakes itself loose, like a prisoner working off a gag? And why should we not shut that pothole up, stuff it full of asphalt, airbrush it gone if it tries to get into the picture?

And if the moon says no? Well, we can put it in anyway, dress it up like a woman who does not want a wedding but must wear brocade white as ice with a train that drags like stones because her mother wants that and she is too afraid, has never stopped being afraid, dies in her bed at eighty-three, having seen the pinched lines around her mother's mouth, as it disapproved the daughter's choice of shrouds? The moon says no? Put it in.

My friends, my fellow Americans, when you go to bed at night, can you change lanes smoothly, without swerves? Are you aware of the speeding car that does not appear in your rear view? Of the unmarked policemen on your either side? I tell you, search your souls. Have you ever truly brought freeways into your life?

# Desire Lines

*When the interstate highway system was designed,
engineers divided the country into a grid, and on the
basis of public hearings and studies, drew "desire lines"
joining the places where people wanted to go.*

There is a line which the wind can erase between
one set of lights on the desert
and another.

There is a line in the air between San Francisco and the pink sky
over the Gulf of Mexico where Tampa Bay
flows into rivers.

There is a line through Pennsylvania, which heaves and buckles
as though it cannot bear to be touched.

There is a Friday night line of flame stretching
from Cleveland to anywhere.

There is a line through Nevada so lonely
no one has found it.

There is a line between the city and the mountains—
any city, any mountains—and, as it climbs,
the long valleys become flutes.

There is a line drawn over ruts, and the tough grasses
that overgrew things cast off in desperation: the child's
music box, the tablecloths, the bones.

There is a line made of paper. If words touch it,
the line will spark from the end, and burn.
End. And burn.

# Acknowledgments

Grateful acknowledgment to the editors/publishers of the books/journals in which these works previously appeared:

• • •

*Planting the Children*, University of Florida Press, © 1983 by Lola Haskins;

*Castings*, Countryman Press, © 1984 by Lola Haskins; 2nd edition, Betony Press, © 1992 by Lola Haskins;

*Across Her Broad Lap Something Wonderful*, State Street Press, © 1989 by Lola Haskins;

*Forty-Four Ambitions for the Piano*, University Press of Florida, © 1990 by Lola Haskins; 2nd edition Betony Press, © 1994 by Lola Haskins;

*Hunger*, University of Iowa Press, © 1993 by Lola Haskins; 2nd edition, Story Line Press, © 1996 by Lola Haskins.

• • •

New Poems:
*Atlantic Monthly*: "Love";
*Beloit Poetry Journal*: "Sleep Positions";
*Brevity*: "Youth";
*Café Review*: "Appoggiatura and Fermata";
*Christian Science Monitor*: "Love Story";
*Connecticut Review*: "Composition";
*Defined Providence*: Daddy's Writing";
*Flyway*: "Night Waking";
*Georgia Review*: "Times," "Desire Lines";
*Kalliope*: "The Composer Interviews Her Piece";
*Massachusetts Review*: "Interstate Dreams";
*Mississippi Review*: "Pastoral";
*Ploughshares*: "Grass";
*Poetry Review* (London): "The Maker of Lines";

*Prairie Schooner:* "Anger: Five Plays," "Words," "You're Dreaming," "Love and Cancer";

*Shenandoah:* "She Drives";

*Snakeskin:* "The Teacher";

*Southern Review:* "Dogwood, December," "Dearborn North Apartments," "The .38";

*Tampa Review:* "For Mother, After the Vision Fire."

• • •

The following poems also appeared in anthologies, whose editors are gratefully acknowledged: "Dearborn North Apartments" in *180: A Turning Back to Poetry* (Random House); "Love" in *Poems to Set You Free* (Warner Books); "Times" in *9mm* (University of Pittsburgh Press); "To Play Pianissimo" and "The Prodigy" in *Mixed Voices* (Milkweed Editions); "Accidentals" in *Always the Beautiful Answer: A Prose Poem Primer* (Kings Estate Press); "At Eighty" in *Women and Death* (Ground Torpedo Press); "To Wear the Veil" and "Secrets of the Fur Trade" in *Anthology of Magazine Verse and Yearbook of American Poetry* (Monitor Book Company); "Things" in *The State Street Reader* (State Street Press); "The .38" in *Snakebird: Thirty Years of Anhinga Poets* (Anhinga Press); "A Confluence" and "The Prodigy" in *Isle of Flowers* (Anhinga Press); "She Drives," "Love," "The Laws of Women," and "Dearborn North Apartments" in *The Kali Guide* (Zenprint); "Winston, you were wrong" and "Cleaning Cotton at Night" in *Florida in Poetry* (Pineapple Press); "The Teacher" in *Postcards from Pottersville* (Pottersville Press).

• • •

The Jane poems in *Castings* were incorporated in *Jane's War*, broadcast on NPR. *Julia's Peace* is forthcoming from the same series. "Dearborn North Apartments" was featured on NPR's *The Writer's Almanac*, read by Garrison Keillor.

• • •

In addition, thanks to the editors of the following on-line sites for posting some of these poems: *The Alsop Review, Poetry Daily, Verse Daily, The Plagiarist,*

*RockSaltPlum, Tripod, Poem-hunter, WGCU, Hogtown Creek, The Third Muse, nea.gov, Ministry of Whimsy, Mind Caviar, The Atlantic, NYQuarterly, Beloit Poetry Journal, Mississippi Review, On-Line Poetry Classroom,* and *Geometry.net.* It was impossible to include all on-line posters, so a general and genuine thanks to everyone who gave screen-space to my work.

• • •

Thanks also to the National Endowment for the Arts, for grants which sustained the writing of some of these poems, and to the MacDowell Colony for quiet space. And thanks to all my sharp-eyed friends, especially Sidney, Joe, Brandy, Andrea and Nick. But the dearest of thanks goes to my family— Gerald, D'Arcy, and Django—for sustaining my heart all these years.

# About the Author

Lola Haskins has published seven previous collections of poetry, most recently *The Rim Benders* (Anhinga, 2001) and *Extranjera* (Story Line, 1998). Her work has appeared in *The Atlantic Monthly, The Christian Science Monitor, The London Review of Books, Beloit Poetry Journal, Georgia Review, Southern Review, Prairie Schooner*, and elsewhere. She has been featured on PBS in the United States and on BBC in England. Her awards include two fellowships from the National Endowment for the Arts, four individual artist fellowships from the state of Florida, the Iowa Poetry Prize, and the Emily Dickinson/Writer Magazine award from the Poetry Society of America. Ms. Haskins enjoys collaborating with other artists. Recent examples include performing *Forty-Four Ambitions for the Piano* with Kevin Sharpe, a classical pianist, and James Paul Sain, an electro-acoustic composer, and playing "the speaking Mata Hari" in a ballet of that title for which she wrote the libretto. Ms. Haskins' day job is teaching Computer Science at the University of Florida. She lives in a house she built with her husband on land outside Gainesville, where the locals include possums, armadillos, deer, and Florida black bears. More of her work can be found at www.lolahaskins.com.

# BOA EDITIONS, LTD.

## AMERICAN POETS CONTINUUM SERIES

# Colophon

*Desire Lines: New and Selected Poems*, by Lola Haskins,
was set in Bembo by Richard Foerster, York Beach, Maine.
The cover design is by Lisa Mauro/Mauro Design, Rochester, New York.
The cover art, entitled "Japonesque," is by Norman Jensen.
Manufacturing was by McNaughton & Gunn, Saline, Michigan.

The publication of this book was made possible in part by the special
support of the following individuals:

Nancy & Alan Cameros
J. Christine Wilson & Mary K. Collins
Dr. & Mrs. Gary H. Conners
Burch & Louise Craig
Susan De Witt Davie
Brooks DuBose
Suzanne & Peter Durant
Dr. Henry & Beverly French
Bob & Rae Gilson
Judy & Dane Gordon
Kip & Deb Hale
Peter & Robin Hursh
Robert & Willy Hursh
Archie & Pat Kutz
Rosemary & Lew Lloyd
Dr. Timothy & Penelope Quill
Boo Poulin
Deborah Ronnen
N. Colwell Snell
Celia Jane Stuart-Powles
Janet Tyler
Ellen P. Wallack
Pat & Michael Wilder